ALTERNATOR BOOKS™

MYSTERIES OF
MACHU PICCHU

Elizabeth Weitzman

Lerner Publications ◆ Minneapolis

For Eric and Eva

Lerner Publications Company
A division of Lerner Publishing Group, Inc.
241 First Avenue North
Minneapolis, MN 55401 USA

For reading levels and more information, look up this title at www.lernerbooks.com.

Main body text set in Aptifer Slab LT Pro Regular 11.5/18.
Typeface provided by Linotype AG.

Library of Congress Cataloging-in-Publication Data

Names: Weitzman, Elizabeth, author.
Title: Mysteries of Machu Picchu / Elizabeth Weitzman.
Description: Minneapolis : Lerner Publications, [2017] | Series: Ancient mysteries | Includes bibliographical references and index.
Identifiers: LCCN 2016042654 (print) | LCCN 2016044232 (ebook) | ISBN 9781512440188 (library bound : alkaline paper) | ISBN 9781512449181 (eb pdf)
Subjects: LCSH: Machu Picchu Site (Peru)—Juvenile literature. | Incas—Juvenile literature.
Classification: LCC F3429.1.M3 W45 2017 (print) | LCC F3429.1.M3 (ebook) | DDC 985/.37—dc23

LC record available at https://lccn.loc.gov/2016042654

Manufactured in the United States of America
1-42280-26137-1/20/2017

TABLE OF CONTENTS

INTRODUCTION
THE SEARCH BEGINS

Hiram Bingham crawled up the side of a mountain on his hands and knees. He barely noticed the rain falling all around him. He didn't even care that there were poisonous snakes nearby.

The American explorer had arrived in Peru's Andes Mountains in July 1911. He had already crossed thundering rapids on a wobbly bridge. He'd thrashed through thick tropical forests. And he was climbing cliffs steep enough to send him crashing thousands of feet down with just one misstep.

Bingham stands in Pampaconas, Peru, during his 1911 exploration in the Andes Mountains.

Why would anyone put himself in so much danger? Bingham had learned about the forgotten cities of Peru's ancient **Inca** people while he was teaching at Yale University in Connecticut. He decided he wanted to find some of the cities, especially Vilcabamba, the last Inca city that was taken over by **conquistadores**. Then, while searching for the ancient ruins, Bingham heard about a lost city hidden somewhere high amid the clouds. But only a few living in the Andes seemed to know about it. Did this mythical place really exist?

Bingham and his team camped in the Andes Mountains during the 1911 expedition.

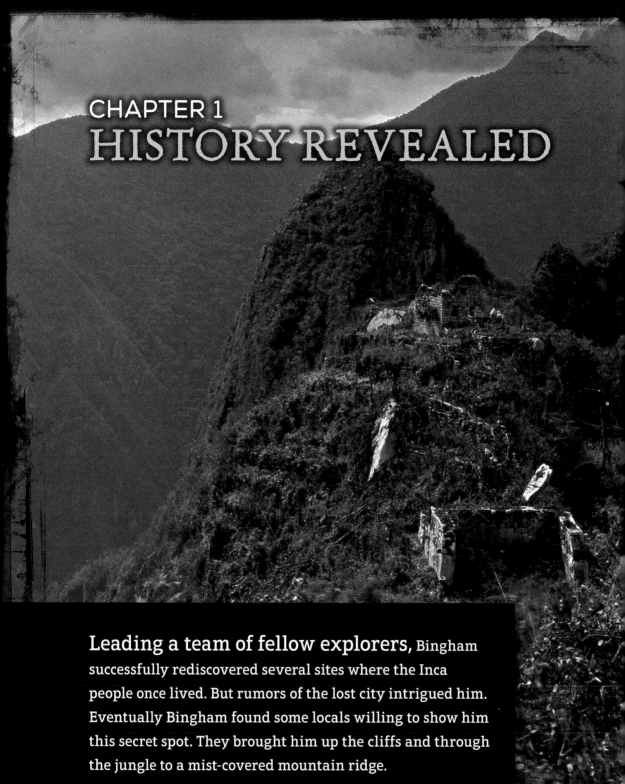

CHAPTER 1
HISTORY REVEALED

Leading a team of fellow explorers, Bingham successfully rediscovered several sites where the Inca people once lived. But rumors of the lost city intrigued him. Eventually Bingham found some locals willing to show him this secret spot. They brought him up the cliffs and through the jungle to a mist-covered mountain ridge.

The ancient stone city of
Machu Picchu

BEAUTIFUL RUINS

What Bingham saw was more thrilling than he could
have ever imagined. Here before him was an entire
city made of stone. It was overgrown but still in good
condition. The city blended in perfectly with the
mountain landscape, built in several levels connected
by paths and stone steps. There seemed to be temples,
fountains, houses, storage buildings, and even places to
study the sky.

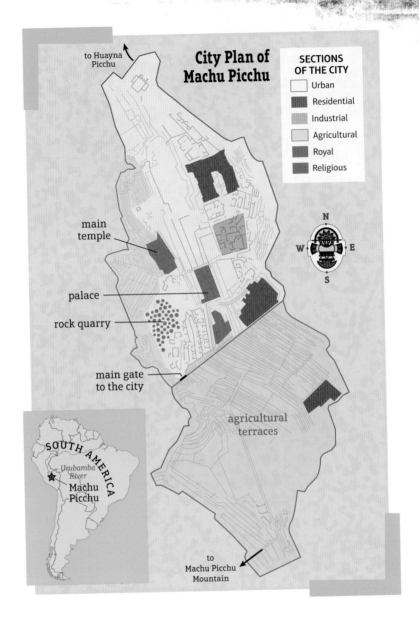

City Plan of Machu Picchu

SECTIONS OF THE CITY
- Urban
- Residential
- Industrial
- Agricultural
- Royal
- Religious

to Huayna Picchu

N
W — E
S

main temple

palace

rock quarry

main gate to the city

agricultural terraces

SOUTH AMERICA
Urubamba River
Machu Picchu

to Machu Picchu Mountain

This, Bingham's guides explained, was Machu Picchu. Machu Picchu means "old peak" in the Inca language of Quechua. The city sits 7,972 feet (2,430 meters) above sea level, near the Inca capital city of Cuzco, on a flat range between the Machu Picchu and Huayna Picchu Mountains.

It is surrounded on three sides by the mighty Urubamba River, which runs 2,000 feet (610 m) below the city. And Machu Picchu is completely invisible from below, which explains why so few people knew of the city.

Who could have created such a special place? How did they build it? What was it used for? And why was it so quickly abandoned?

Huayna Picchu stands behind the city of Machu Picchu.

CHAPTER 2
AN INCREDIBLE EMPIRE

The Inca people who built Machu Picchu established one of the most amazing empires in history. One of the most influential rulers of the Inca was Emperor Pachacuti. His name meant "he who remakes the world," and his goal was to expand the borders of the empire by conquering the surrounding lands and people. At the height of its power, the Inca Empire spanned the western edge of South America from Ecuador to Chile. Their roadway system stretched across approximately 25,000 miles (40,234 kilometers) of the empire, they had complex **architecture**, and they built systems for **irrigating** crops. The Inca people believed in several gods, and temples and shrines were common throughout the empire. Priests had a central role in Inca life. The Inca people did not have a written language but had a common spoken language to pass down stories throughout generations.

An Incan irrigation system, used to water terraced crops

A royal Inca tunic, or item of clothing, from Machu Picchu was on display at Yale University in 2003.

Much about Machu Picchu is still a puzzle. But archaeologists have learned a lot about the city from historical clues. The Spanish soldiers who later conquered the empire left detailed records about Inca culture. Stories have been passed down to people still living in the Andes. And there is also much to be learned from the ruins themselves, as well as from **artifacts** Bingham brought back to Yale University.

MYTH ALERT!

Bingham discovered a large group of skeletons at Machu Picchu. He thought that the skeletons were all female and that Machu Picchu must have been a place where a group of women lived who were dedicated to the Inca sun god and took part in religious ceremonies. But modern tests have shown that half the skeletons Bingham found were male! So the chosen women may not have lived there at all.

Historians and archaeologists have come up with many theories about the purpose of Machu Picchu. Some believe that the city was a prison. Others have theorized that the city was a military stronghold. Some think it may have been a place to test crops. One theory even suggests aliens came to Earth to build the city.

THE ROYAL ESTATE

Many modern scholars believe that Pachacuti built Machu Picchu to be a royal estate or retreat—a place for rulers to rest between conquests. Similar royal Inca estates have been uncovered in other parts of Peru.

And the presence of royal buildings in Machu Picchu backs up the theory. These buildings were used by the emperor and his family. The emperor's home had a garden as well as a private bath and toilet. These seem to be the only private quarters in the city. The rest of the city might have been inhabited year-round by caretakers of the buildings and farmland.

Historians and archaeologists continue working at Machu Picchu to preserve and learn more about the ancient city.

DIG DEEP

In Inca culture, leaders were honored forever. When they died, they were turned into mummies, or *mallquis*. Archaeological digs have uncovered some of these mummies. From the way they were buried, it is clear that these mallquis were treated with great care. They stayed in special tombs and caves and were given the finest clothes. Historians also found that the mallquis were brought out to appear at religious ceremonies and even traveled from place to place with their families.

A Peruvian archaeologist discusses a mummy uncovered in an Incan cemetery.

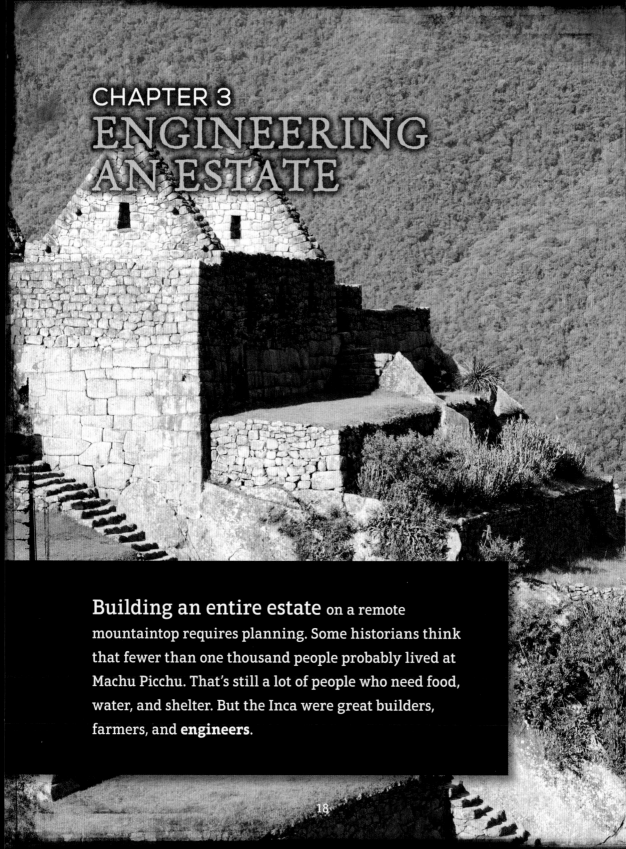

CHAPTER 3
ENGINEERING AN ESTATE

Building an entire estate on a remote mountaintop requires planning. Some historians think that fewer than one thousand people probably lived at Machu Picchu. That's still a lot of people who need food, water, and shelter. But the Inca were great builders, farmers, and **engineers**.

Machu Picchu was carefully organized. The city covered a 5-mile (8 km) area and was separated into sections for farming, housing, religious practice, and royal buildings. The different areas and levels of the city were connected by three thousand stone steps. On these different levels, or terraces, crops such as corn and potatoes were grown. Farming on terraces helped to preserve soil and save water. These methods kept the land from **eroding**. A system of fountains distributed water to the various levels of the city.

Agricultural terraces beyond the city of Machu Picchu

DIG DEEP

Ground-penetrating radar (GPR) has helped archaeologists understand much more about Machu Picchu's foundations. The equipment sends pulses of energy into the earth to identify the depth, size, and texture of materials underground. GPR has discovered deep drainage systems of rocks and soil beneath the buildings and terraces at Machu Picchu. These made the land strong enough to build on and the terraces sturdy enough to grow food on.

SACRED STRUCTURES

The structure of Machu Picchu also reflects the culture and religion of the Inca people. Archaeologists believe that each major structure in the city was designed to honor or examine nature. The main entrance to Machu Picchu is a gate that carefully frames the Huayna Picchu Mountain. And both the Temple of the Sun and the Temple of the Three Windows were built so that sunlight streams through them on the longest and shortest days of the year.

The Temple of the Sun was built at the highest point of the city. Important events and rituals took place here.

A large, carved rock known as the Intihuatana stone was used to track the sun. But the Inca people also believed the stone was a door to another realm. According to legend, some people could talk with spirits if they touched their foreheads to the stone.

These **sacred** structures were also useful. By studying the sky, the Inca were able to create a calendar. The sun and moon told them when it was time to plant crops, when to return to their capital city before the rainy season, and when to pray for good weather or ask the gods to give them a strong growing season.

The Intihuatana stone

A building in the housing area of Machu Picchu shows how well the stone blocks fit together.

Everything in the city was made of stone from a local rock quarry. The Inca didn't have wheels, so archaeologists think they pulled the huge stones on wooden rollers. Then they lifted them up into place with long levers. The Inca people carefully chiseled, shaped, and polished the stones. Without modern tools or technology, one way they cut rocks was by pounding them with smaller, harder stones. And these rocks were cut to fit together perfectly—they didn't even need mortar or cement to stay in place. The structures were built so well that they have survived for more than five hundred years.

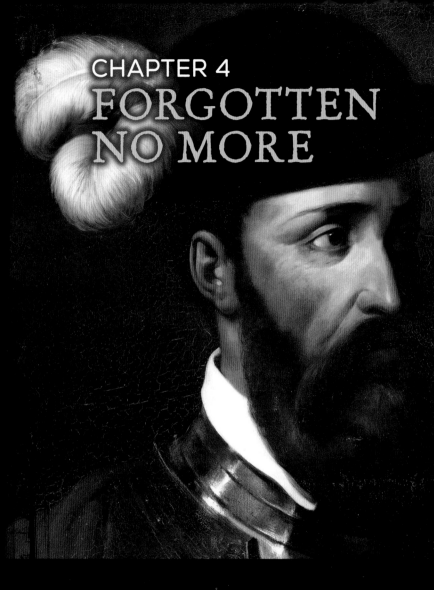

CHAPTER 4
FORGOTTEN
NO MORE

In 1532 Spanish conquistador Francisco Pizarro arrived from Spain. He wanted to claim Peru and its treasures for his own country. That meant destroying the culture and people who were already there. The Inca armies were no match for Spanish soldiers, and diseases introduced by the Spanish killed many people in the Andes. Over the next forty years, contact with the Spanish brought the end of the Inca Empire—and of Machu Picchu.

Pizarro and his troops tore through the country. They made detailed records of what they found and what they destroyed. But there is no mention *at all* of Machu Picchu. It seems the Spanish never even knew about one of the greatest cultural marvels in history.

Historians aren't entirely sure when or why the city was deserted. Some believe the city was occupied for one hundred years before being abandoned. One idea is that the people abandoned the city to please the gods after their emperor died. But it's likely that it became too hard to keep up the roads and buildings as disease and war ravaged the empire. And so this incredible creation disappeared into the mountains.

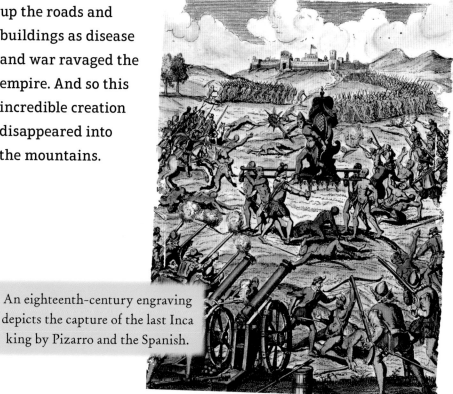

An eighteenth-century engraving depicts the capture of the last Inca king by Pizarro and the Spanish.

PROTECTING A LEGACY

Four centuries later, Bingham brought Machu Picchu
back into the open. And the world has been fascinated
by this rediscovered treasure ever since. In 2007 it
was voted one of the New Seven Wonders of the World,
and it has become a popular tourism destination.
Every year one million people walk across the terraces
and run their hands along the stone. Many still view
Machu Picchu as a sacred site—a place to get healing
or energy. The estate was made to withstand wind and
rain. But tourism is another matter.

In recent years, scientists and citizens have worked
together to protect the area. In 1983 the United Nations
Educational, Scientific and Cultural Organization

Tourists participate
in a ceremony at the
Intihuatana stone.

(UNESCO) declared Machu Picchu a World Heritage Site, an important site that deserves to be protected. Since then people have become more aware of how important and fragile it really is.

And in 2011, Yale University returned to Peru many of the items Bingham had brought back to the United States. They are on display in a museum in Cuzco. We may never know everything about Machu Picchu. But through stories, tourism, and artifacts, this once-sacred site lives on, leaving people inspired and in awe of the city hidden in the clouds.

MYTH ALERT!

Bingham is generally believed to be the first person to discover Machu Picchu after it was abandoned by the Inca. However, there is evidence that other explorers and missionaries had visited this mysterious site earlier. Three treasure hunters signed their names on a rock in the city, and some say there may have even been families living at Machu Picchu when Bingham arrived!

SCIENCE SPOTLIGHT
OSTEOLOGY

Osteology is the study of skeletons. Osteologists have examined ancient Inca bones, looking for clues about life at Machu Picchu. By looking at X-rays of teeth, scientists have found evidence of cavities. That means people living at Machu Picchu may have eaten a lot of sugary maize, or corn. Few broken bones and minimal skull damage shows that these Inca did not fight many battles. And their bones were strong, which means they lived fairly healthy lives. This suggests that rather than a few people doing backbreaking work, many people probably worked together at a steady pace for a long time to build and farm at Machu Picchu.

Timeline

1438	Inca emperor Pachacuti begins his reign. Machu Picchu is built in the mid-fifteenth century.
1471	Pachacuti dies, and his son Túpac Inca Yupanqui takes over. Machu Picchu continues to expand under Túpac's reign.
1532	Francisco Pizarro and his Spanish conquistadores invade Peru.
1572	Conquistadores kill Túpac Amaru, the last Inca leader. By now, Machu Picchu has been abandoned.
1911	Local Peruvians show Hiram Bingham where Machu Picchu is. He tells the world about its marvels.
1983	UNESCO deems Machu Picchu a World Heritage Site.
2007	Machu Picchu is voted one of the New Seven Wonders of the World.
2011	Yale University returns most of the artifacts Bingham brought back from Machu Picchu. They are put on display at the Machu Picchu Museum in Cuzco, Peru.

GLOSSARY

architecture: the design of buildings

artifacts: handmade objects, often discovered during an archaeological dig

conquistadores: sixteenth-century Spanish conquerors of Latin America

engineers: people who design or plan large projects

eroding: being destroyed or worn down by water and wind

Inca: a member of the indigenous peoples who lived in Peru before the Spanish conquest

irrigating: supplying water to land or crops using artificial means, such as pipes

sacred: holy

FURTHER INFORMATION

Burgan, Michael. *Ancient Inca*. New York: Children's Press, 2012.

Historic Sanctuary of Machu Picchu
http://whc.unesco.org/en/list/274

Lewin, Ted. *Lost City: The Discovery of Machu Picchu*. New York: Puffin, 2012.

Machajewski, Sarah. *The Ancient Inca Economy*. New York: PowerKids, 2016.

Machu Picchu
http://www.history.com/topics/machu-picchu

Owings, Lisa. *Peru*. Minneapolis: Bellwether Media, 2012.

Sacred Sites: Machu Picchu
https://sacredsites.com/americas/peru/machu_picchu.html

Waxman, Laura Hamilton. *Mysteries of Easter Island*. Minneapolis: Lerner Publications, 2018.

INDEX

PHOTO ACKNOWLEDGMENTS

The images in this book are used with the permission of: © Gordan/Shutterstock.com (grunge frame throughout); © 50Centimos/photocase.com, p. 1; © iStockphoto.com/rchphoto, pp. 4–5; The Granger Collection, New York, pp. 6, 7, 8; © Jarnogz/Dreamstime.com, p. 9; © Laura Westlund/Independent Picture Service, p. 10; © Galyna Andrushko/Dreamstime.com, p. 11; © mauritius images GmbH/Alamy, p. 12; © iStockphoto.com/XiFotos, p. 13; AP Photo/Douglas Healey, p. 14; © astudio/Shutterstock.com, p. 16; © ALEJANDRA BRUN/AFP/Getty Images, p. 17; © iStockphoto.com/tankbmb, p. 18; © iStockphoto.com/Hanis, p. 19; Courtesy Thierry Jamin, p. 20; © iStockphoto.com/Patrick_Gijsbers, p. 21; © Juan Manuel Castro Prieto/Agence VU/Redux, p. 22; © Cristina Stoian/Shutterstock.com, p. 23; Wikimedia Commons, p. 24; Sarin Images/The Granger Collection, New York, p. 25; © National Geographic Creative/Alamy, p. 26; MARIANA BAZO/REUTERS/Newscom, p. 28.

Front cover: © 50Centimos/photocase.com.